EVERLASTING GOD

18 WORSHIP SONGS ARRANGED BY PHILLIP KEVEREN

CONTENTS

— PIANO LEVEL —
ELEMENTARY

ISBN 978-1-4768-1448-3

HAL•LEONARD®
CORPORATION

7777 W. BLUEMOUND RD. P.O. BOX 13819 MILWAUKEE, WI 53213

Visit Hal Leonard Online at
www.halleonard.com

Visit Phillip at
www.PHILLIPKEVEREN.com

AGNUS DEI

Words and Music by
MICHAEL W. SMITH
Arranged by Phillip Keveren

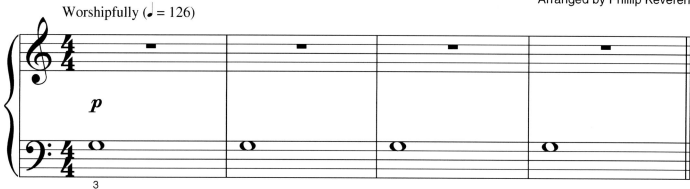

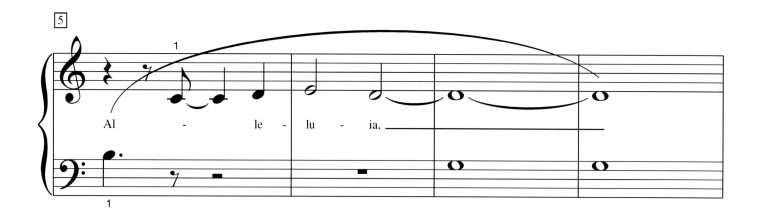

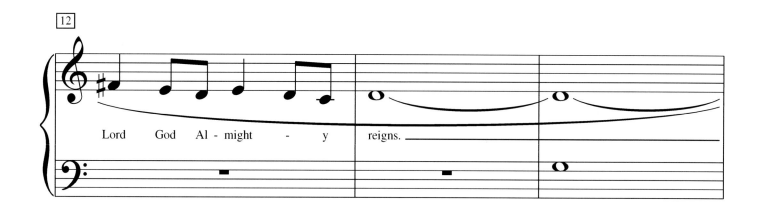

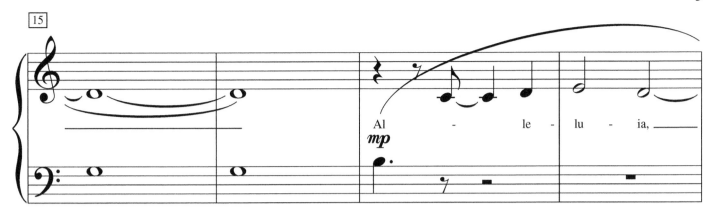

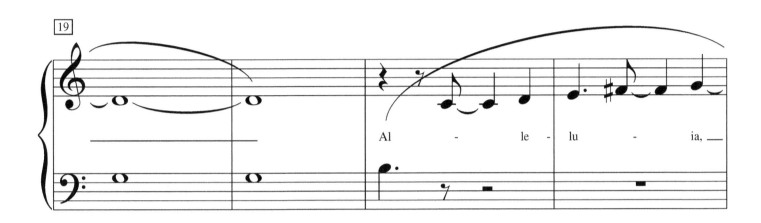

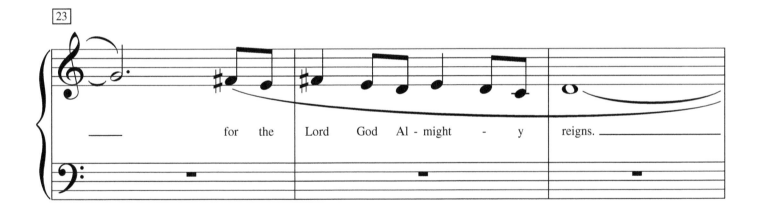

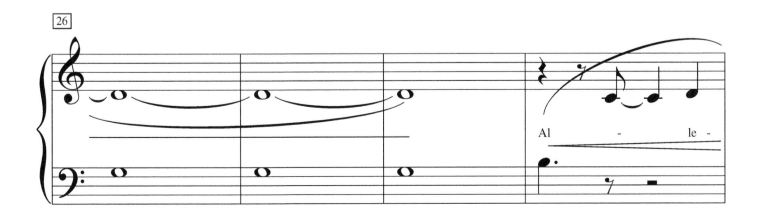

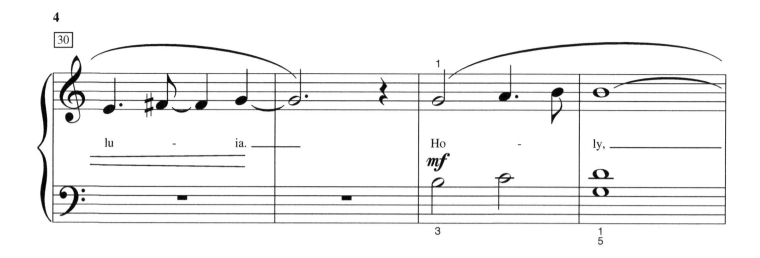

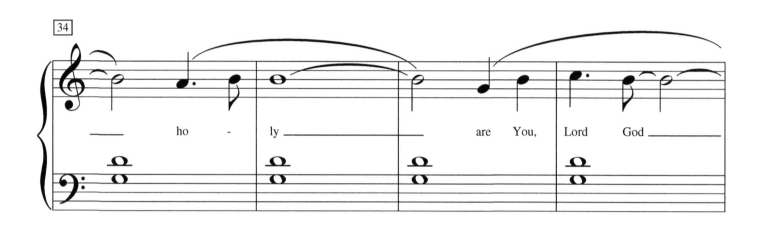

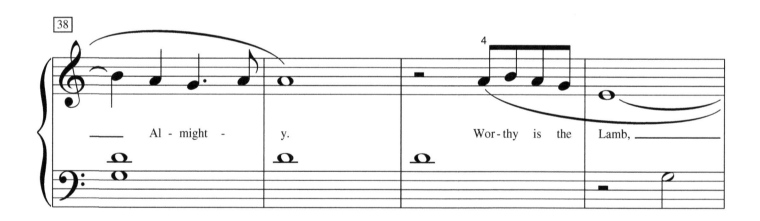

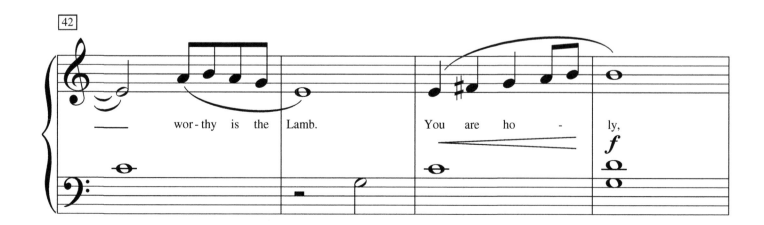

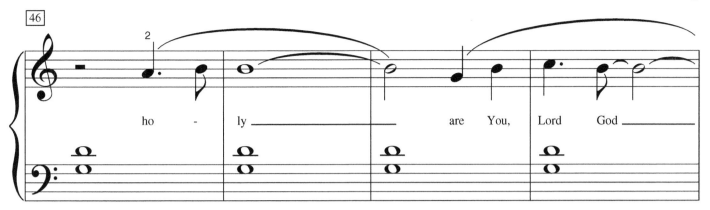

ho - ly _____ are You, Lord God _____

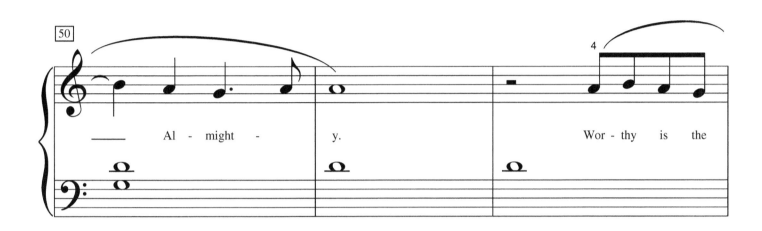

_____ Al - might - y. Wor - thy is the

Lamb, _____ wor - thy is the Lamb. A -

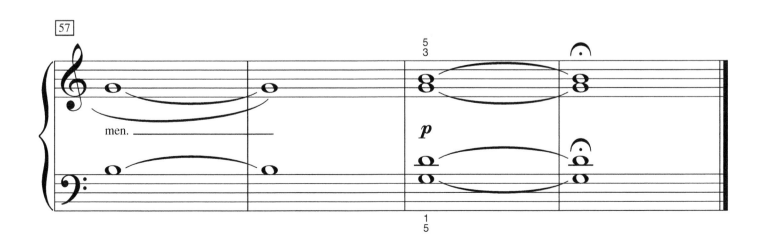

men. _____

Amazing Grace
(My Chains Are Gone)

Words by JOHN NEWTON
Traditional American Melody
Additional Words and Music by CHRIS TOMLIN
and LOUIE GIGLIO
Arranged by Phillip Keveren

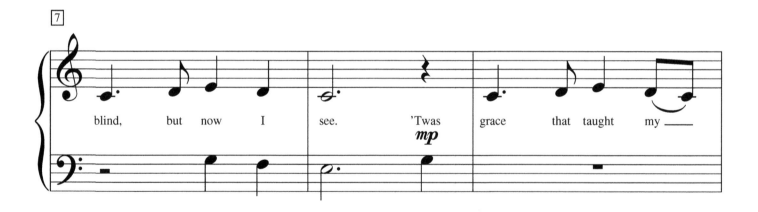

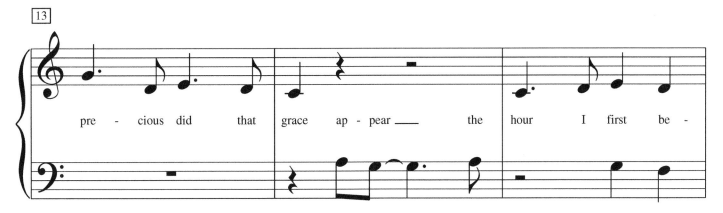

pre - cious did that grace ap - pear ___ the hour I first be -

lieved. My chains are gone, ___ I've been set free. My God, my

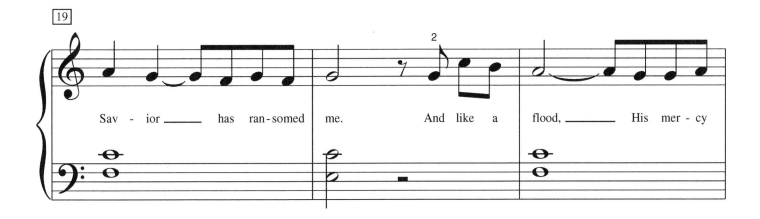

Sav - ior ___ has ran - somed me. And like a flood, ___ His mer - cy

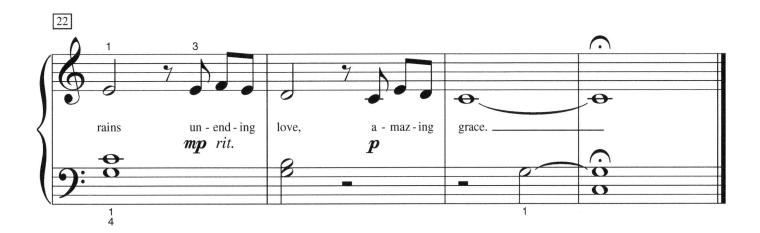

rains un - end - ing love, a - maz - ing grace. ___

AWESOME IS THE LORD MOST HIGH

Words and Music by CHRIS TOMLIN,
JESSE REEVES, CARY PIERCE
and JON ABEL
Arranged by Phillip Keveren

With praise (♩ = 126)

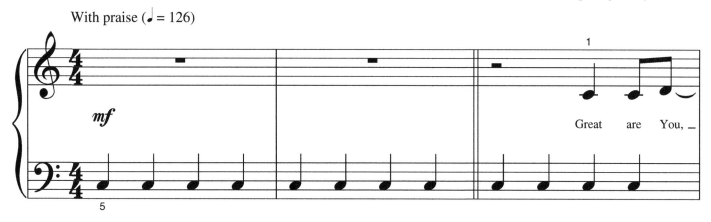

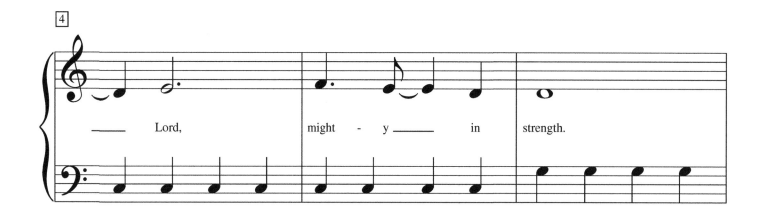

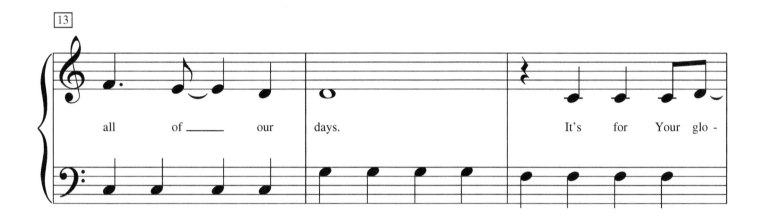

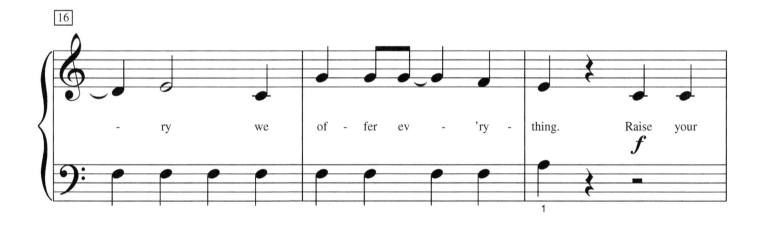

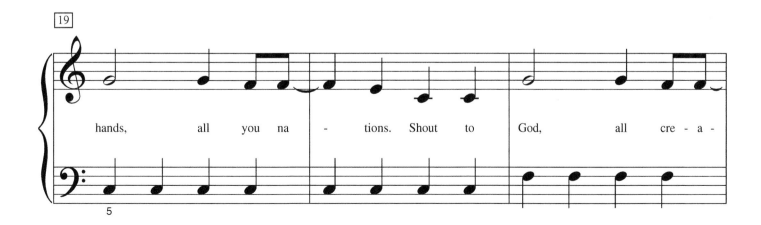

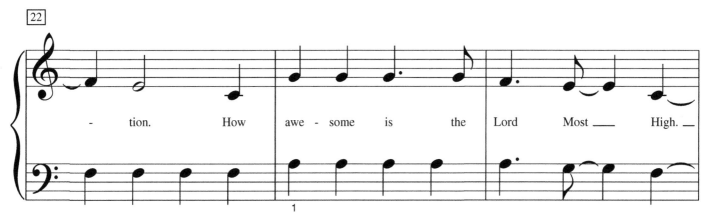

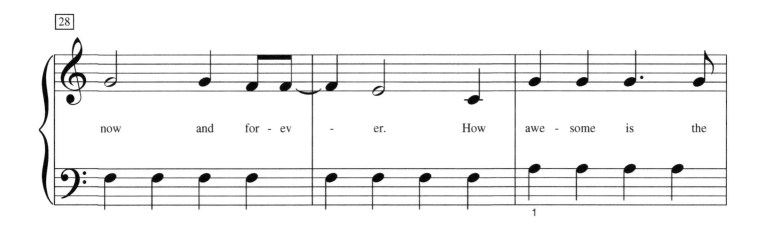

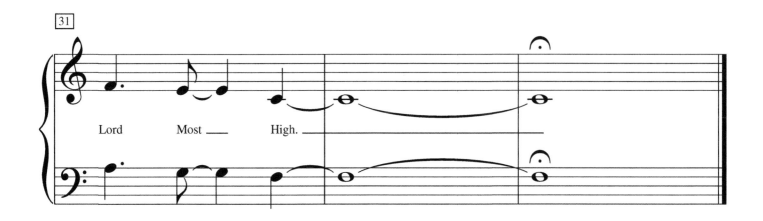

EVERLASTING GOD

Words and Music by BRENTON BROWN
and KEN RILEY
Arranged by Phillip Keveren

With strength (♩ = 120)

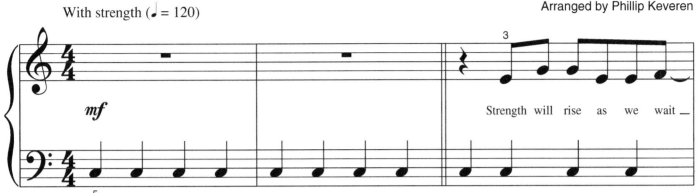

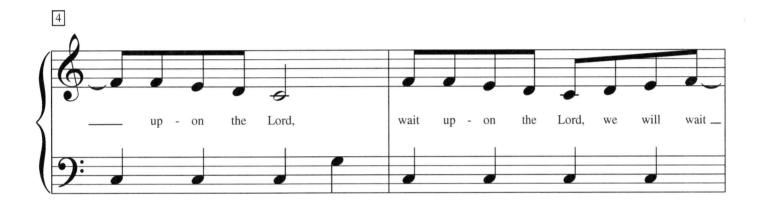

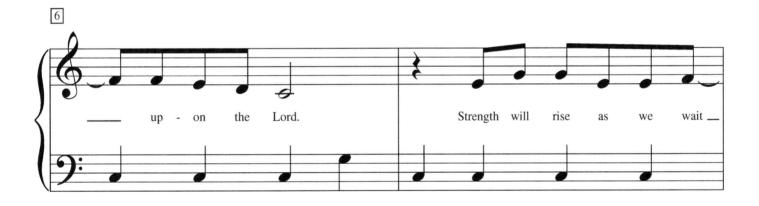

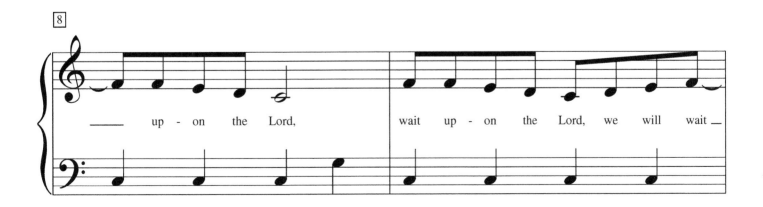

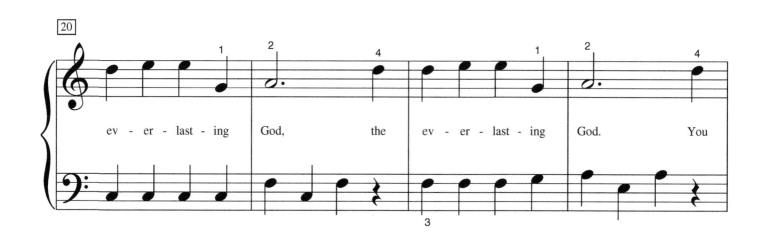

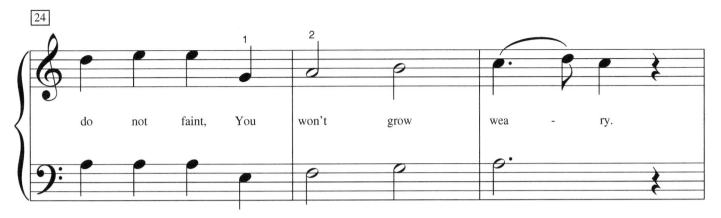

do not faint, You won't grow wea - ry.

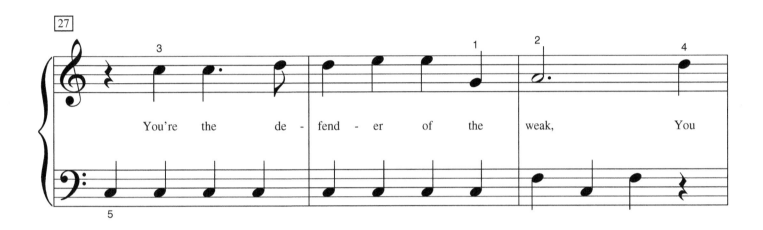

You're the de - fend - er of the weak, You

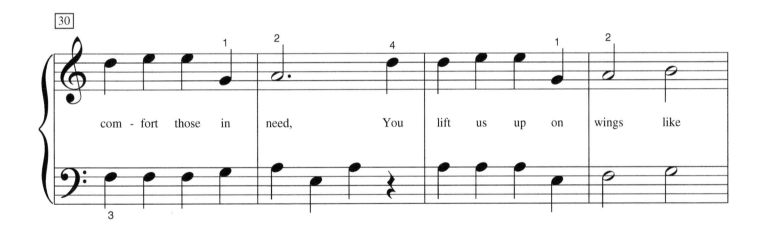

com - fort those in need, You lift us up on wings like

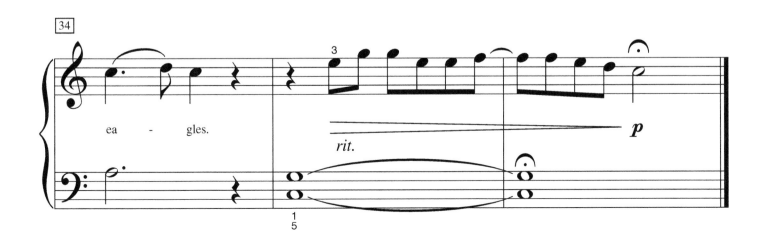

ea - gles.

rit.

p

BLESSED BE YOUR NAME

Words and Music by MATT REDMAN
and BETH REDMAN
Arranged by Phillip Keveren

Flowing (♩ = 132)

mf

Bless - ed be Your name in the land that is

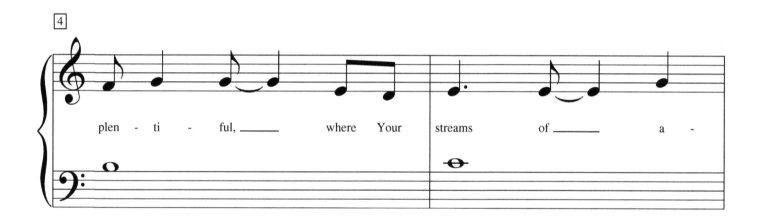

plen - ti - ful, where Your streams of a -

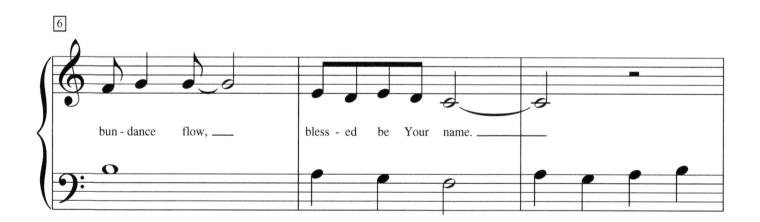

bun - dance flow, bless - ed be Your name.

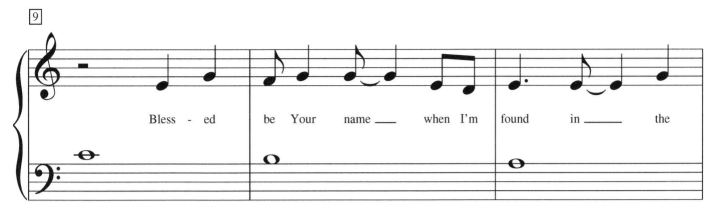

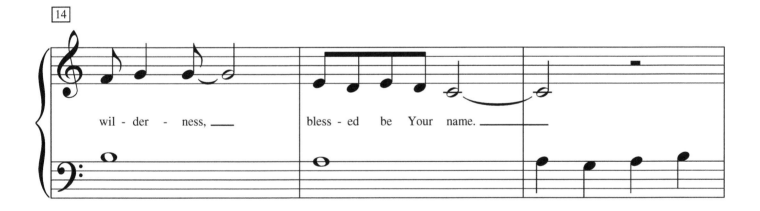

praise.   When the dark-ness   clos-es in, Lord,

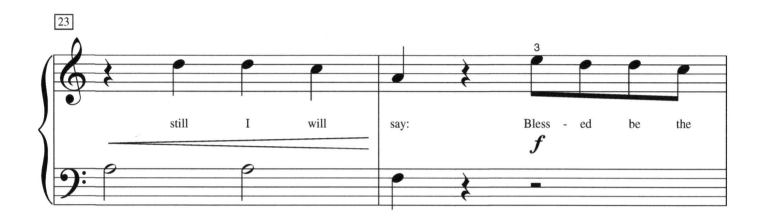

still I will   say: Bless-ed be the

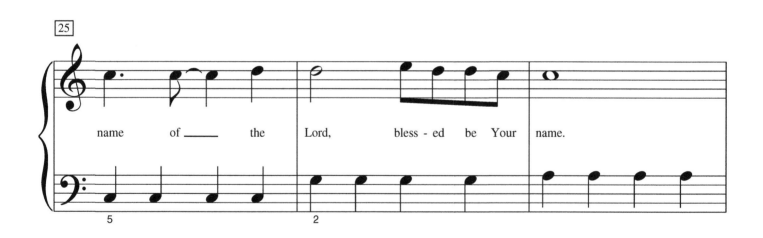

name of ____ the   Lord,   bless-ed be Your   name.

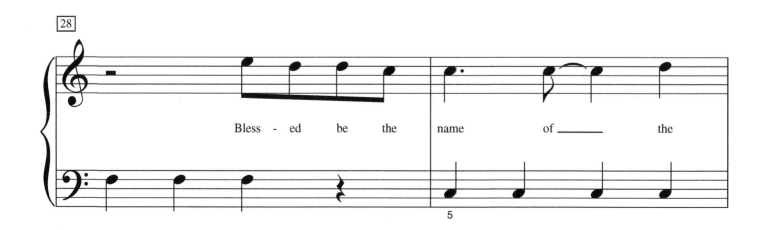

Bless-ed be the   name of ____   the

Lord, bless - ed be Your glo - ri - ous name. You

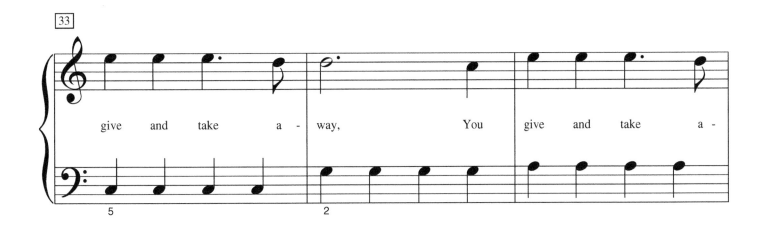

give and take a - way, You give and take a -

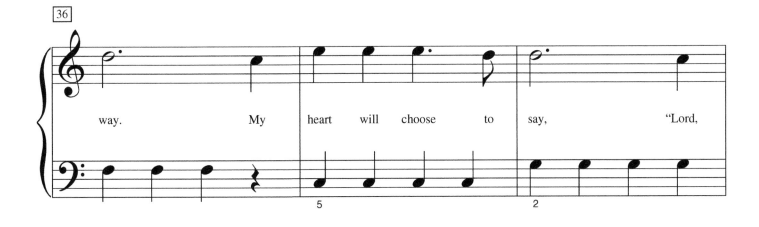

way. My heart will choose to say, "Lord,

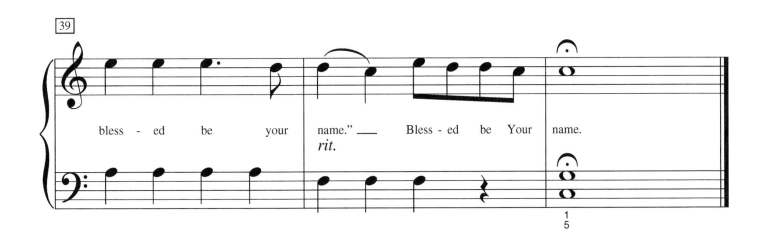

bless - ed be your name." __ Bless - ed be Your name.

rit.

CHRIST IS RISEN

Words and Music by MIA FIELDES
and MATT MAHER
Arranged by Phillip Keveren

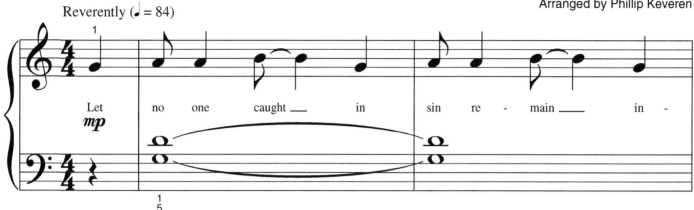

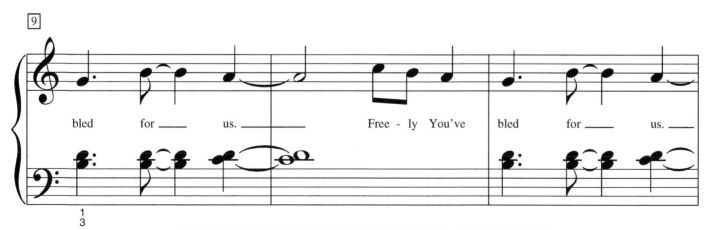

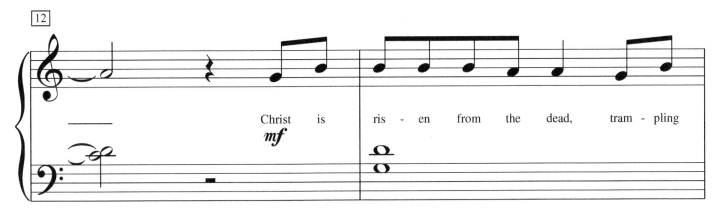

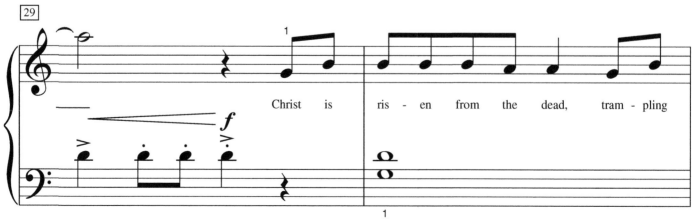

o - ver death by death. Come a - wake, come a - wake, come and

rise up from the grave. Christ is ris - en from the dead; we are

one with Him a - gain. Come a - wake, come a - wake, come and

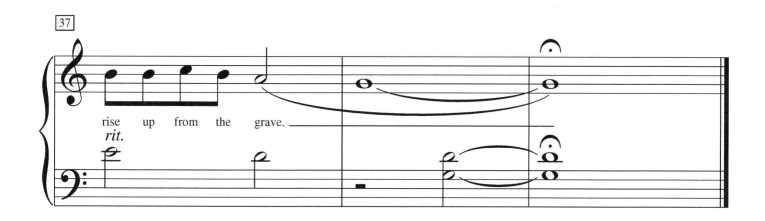

rise up from the grave. _____
rit.

FOREVER REIGN

Words and Music by REUBEN MORGAN
and JASON INGRAM
Arranged by Phillip Keveren

Worshipfully (♩ = 84)

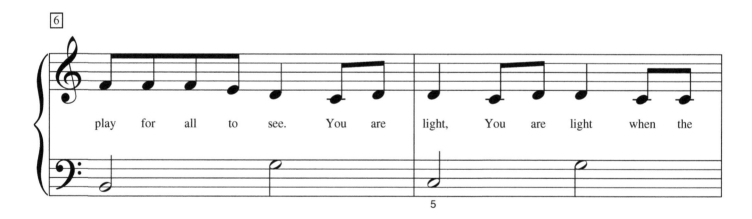

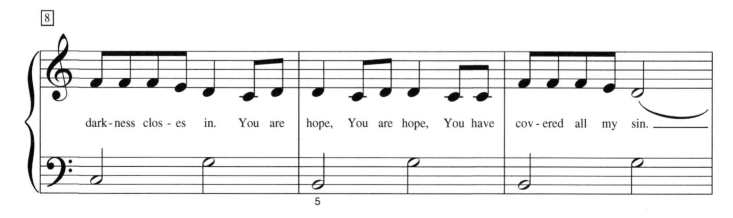

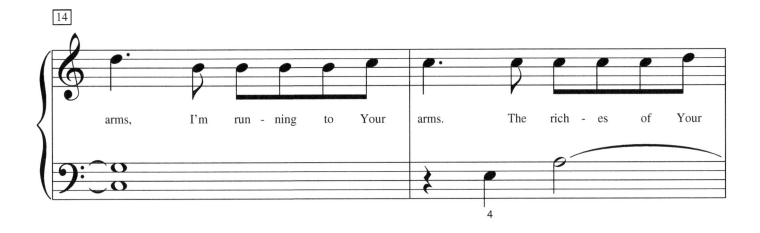

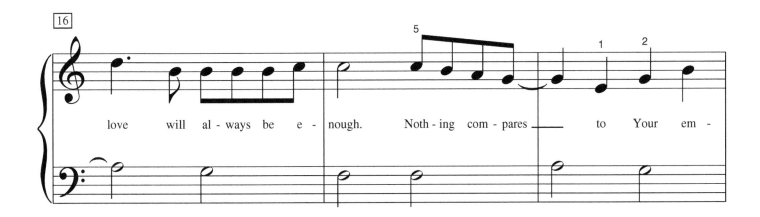

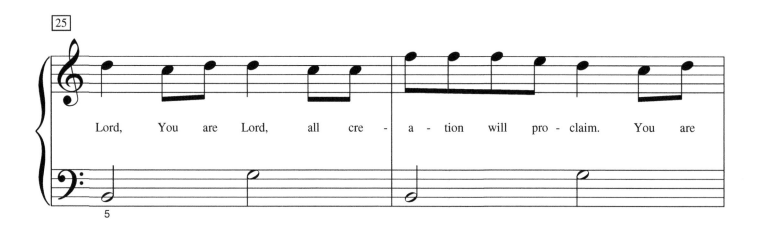

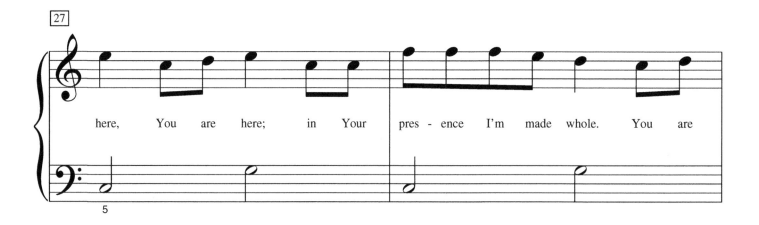

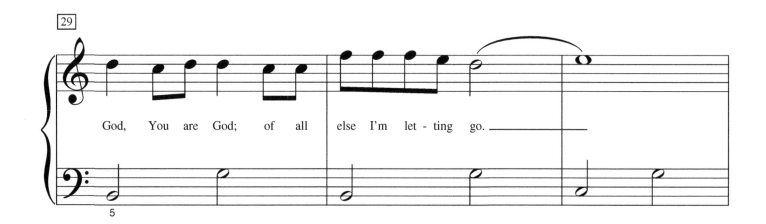

And, oh, I'm run-ning to Your arms, I'm run-ning to Your

arms. The rich - es of Your love will al - ways be e -

nough. Noth - ing com - pares to Your em - brace. Light of the world,

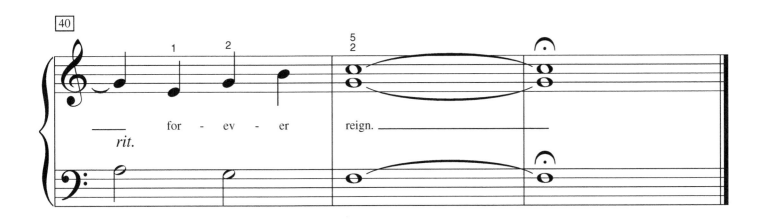

for - ev - er reign.

rit.

FRIEND OF GOD

Words and Music by MICHAEL GUNGOR
and ISRAEL HOUGHTON
Arranged by Phillip Keveren

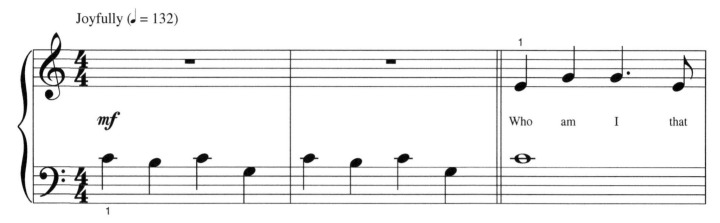

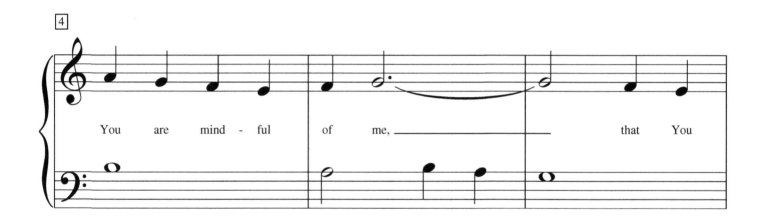

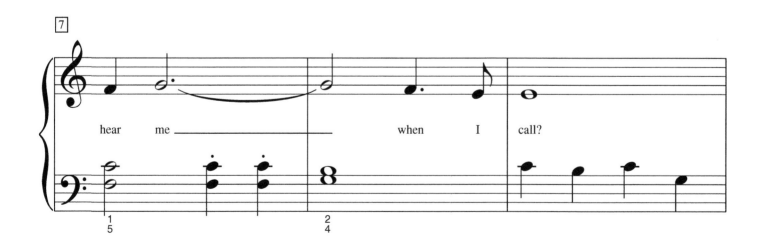

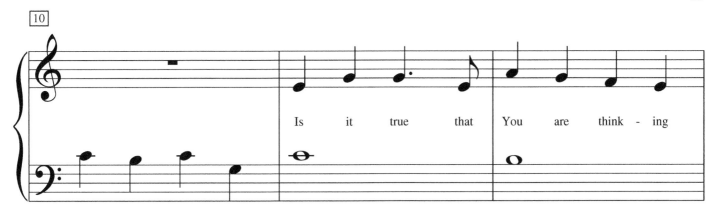

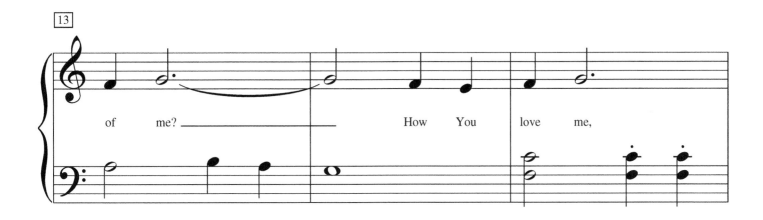

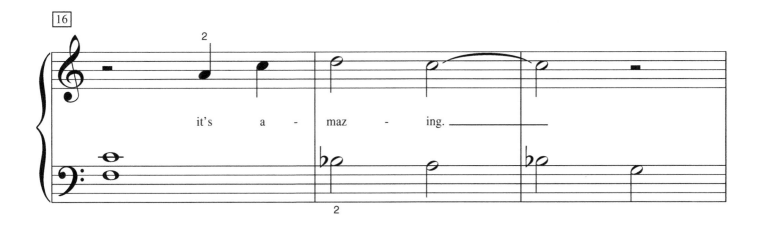

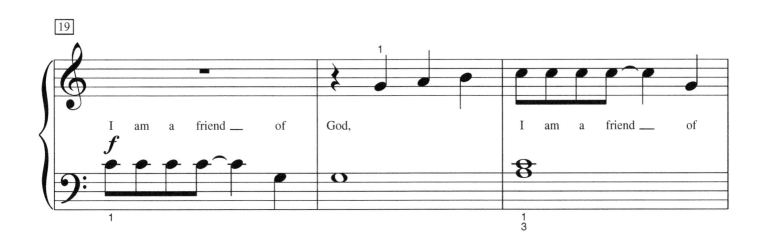

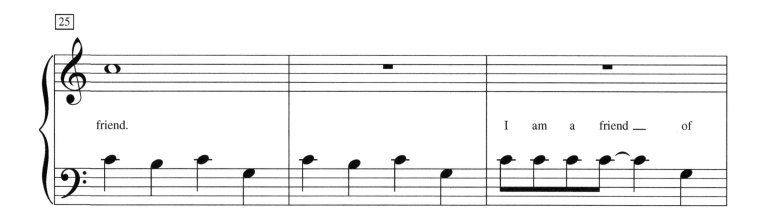

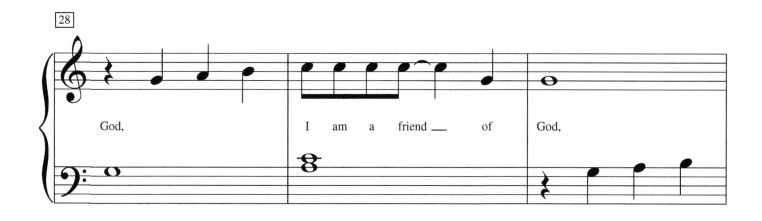

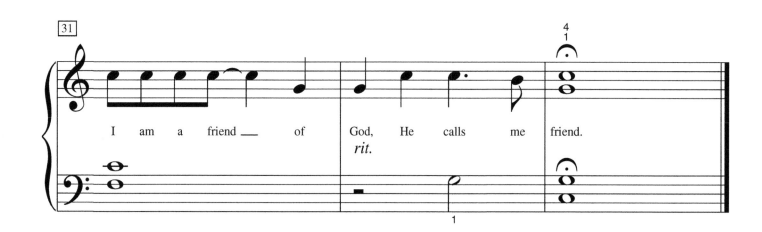

MIGHTY TO SAVE

Words and Music by BEN FIELDING
and REUBEN MORGAN
Arranged by Phillip Keveren

With strength (d = 76)

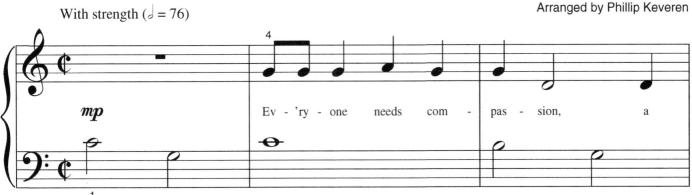

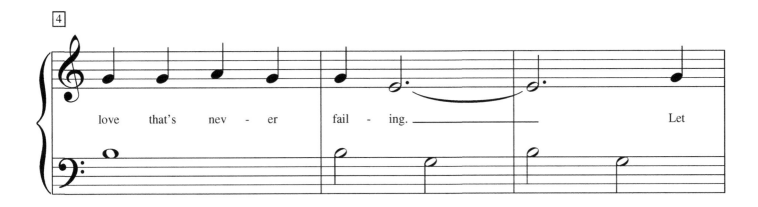

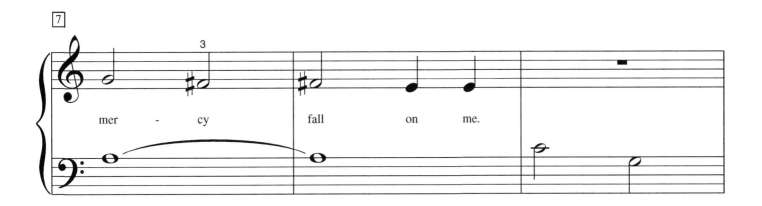

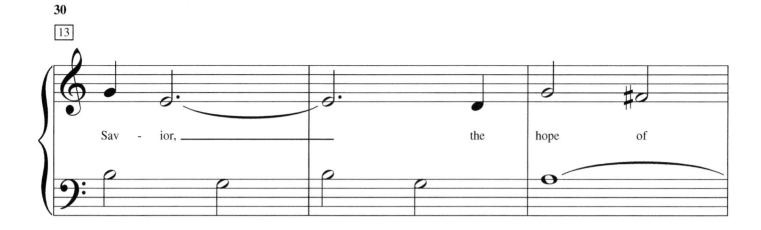

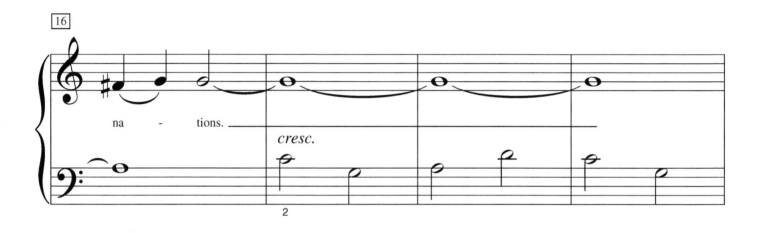

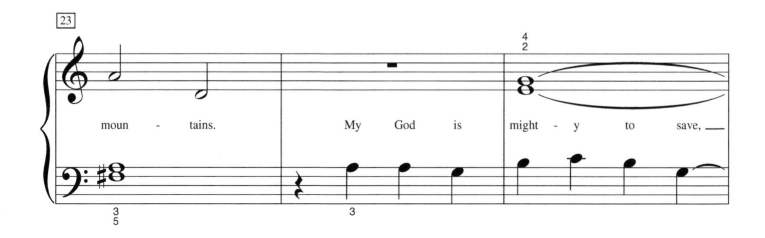

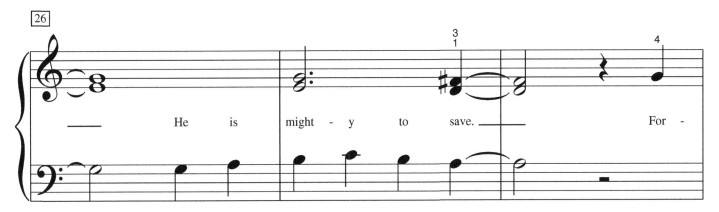

He is might - y to save. _____ For -

ev - er Au - thor of sal - va - tion,

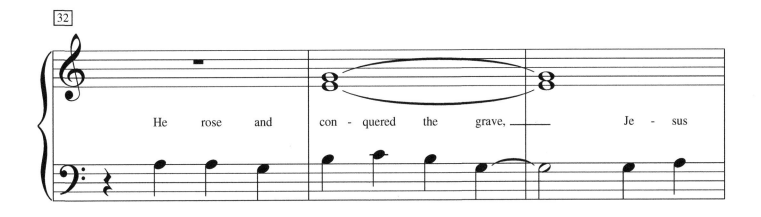

He rose and con - quered the grave, _____ Je - sus

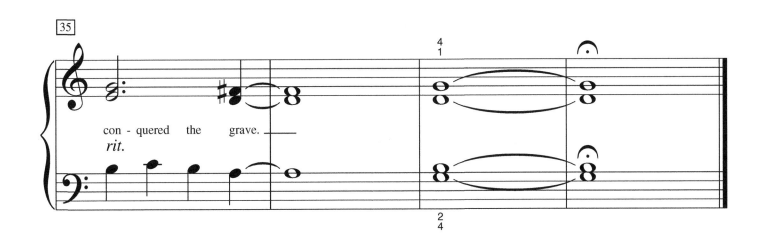

con - quered the grave.
rit.

HERE I AM TO WORSHIP

Words and Music by
TIM HUGHES
Arranged by Phillip Keveren

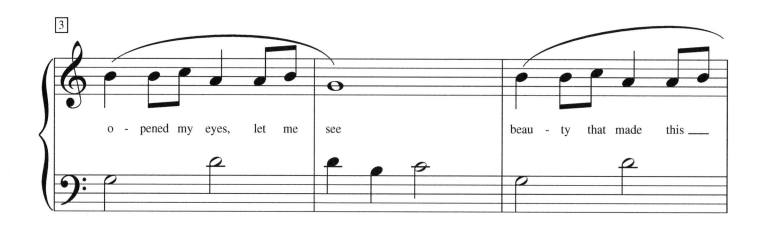

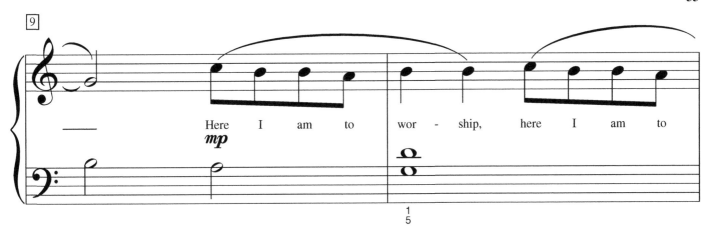

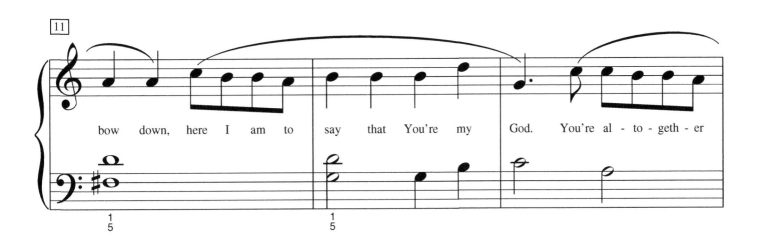

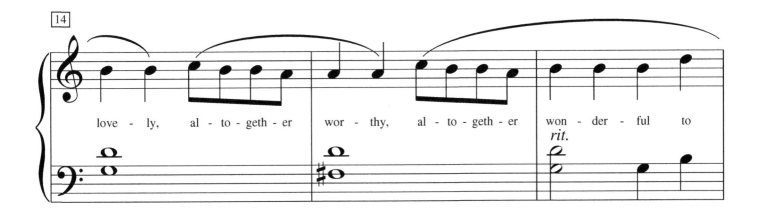

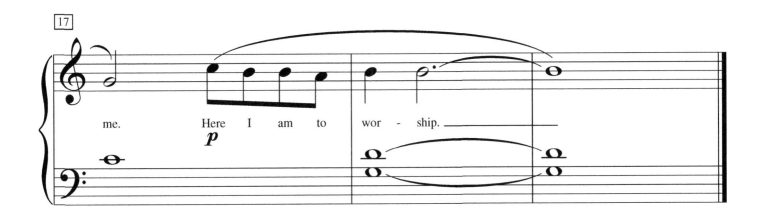

HOSANNA
(Praise Is Rising)

Words and Music by PAUL BALOCHE
and BRENTON BROWN
Arranged by Phillip Keveren

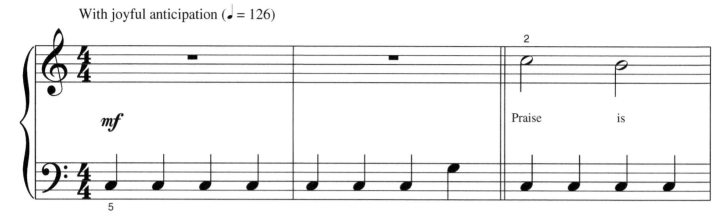

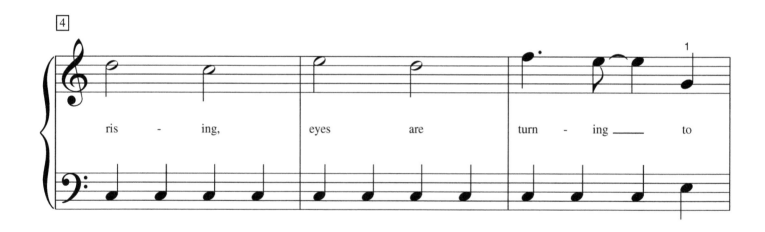

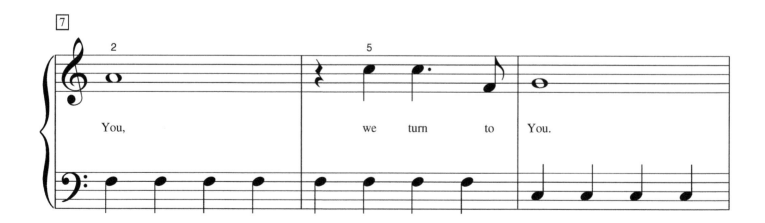

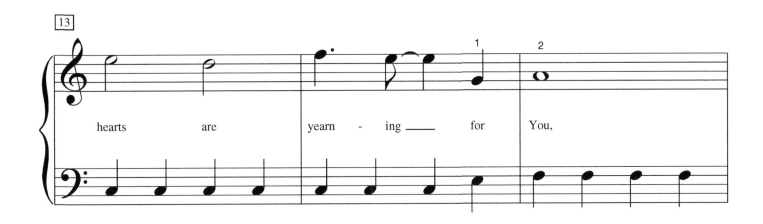

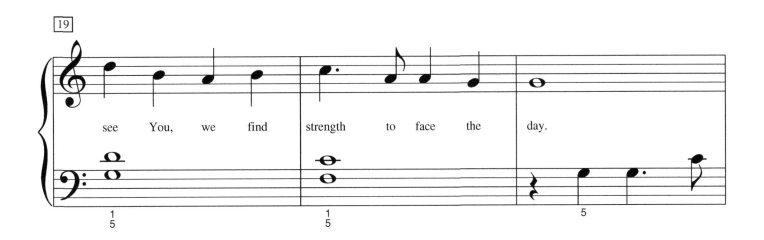

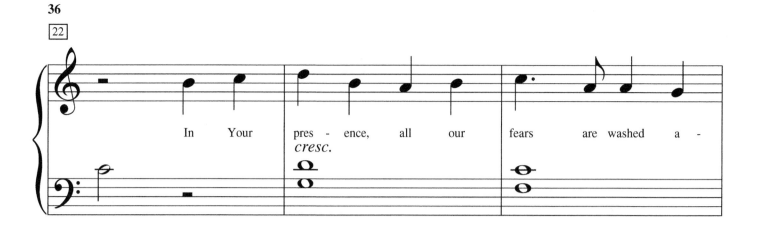

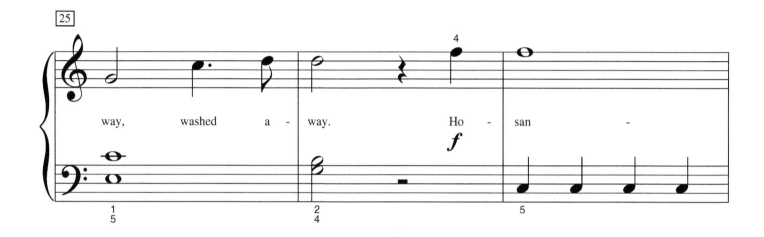

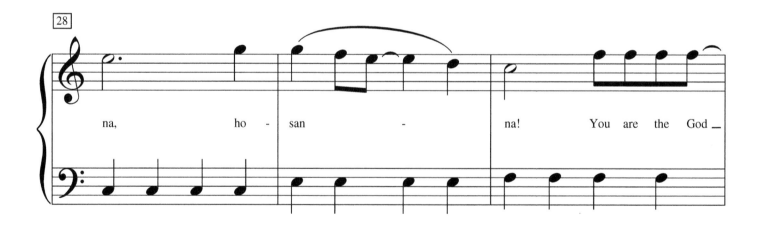

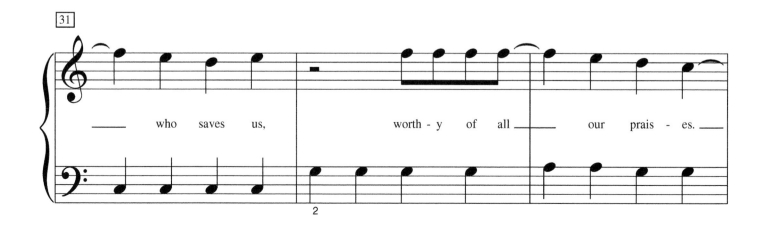

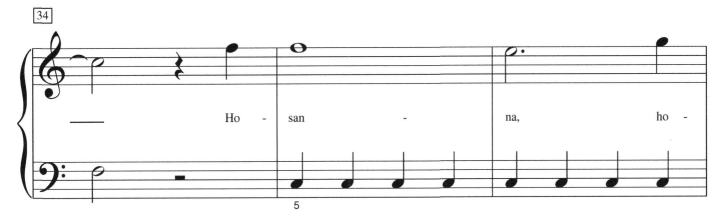

Ho - san - na, ho -

san - na! Come, have Your way __ a - mong us.

We wel - come You here, __ Lord Je - sus. __ Ho -

rit.

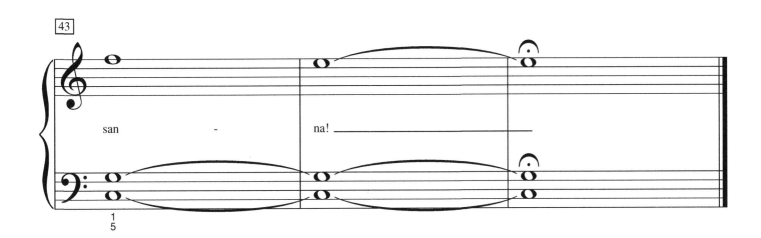

san - na! __

HOW GREAT IS OUR GOD

Words and Music by CHRIS TOMLIN,
JESSE REEVES and ED CASH
Arranged by Phillip Keveren

With wonder (♩ = 108)

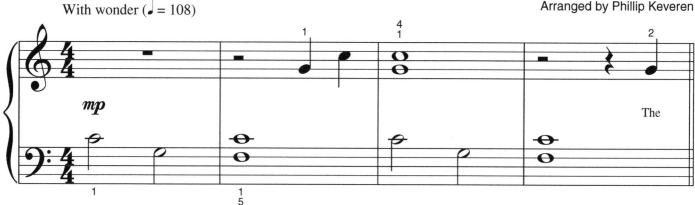

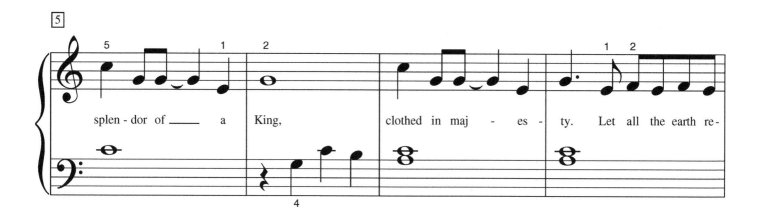

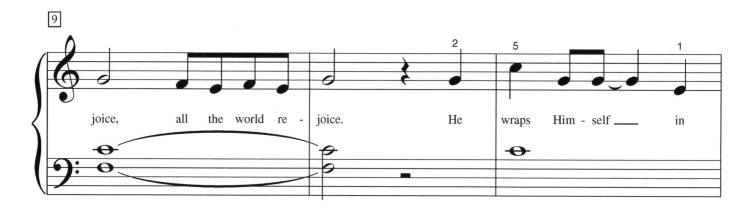

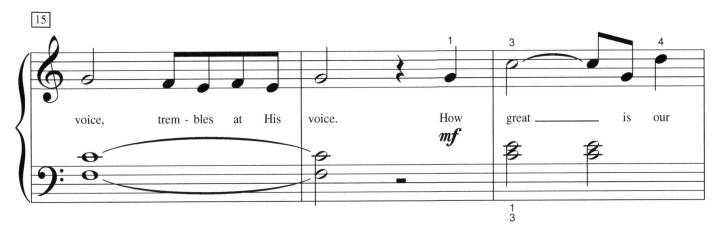

voice, trem - bles at His voice. How great _____ is our

mf

God! Sing with me: How great _____ is our God! And all will see how

great, how great _____ is our God!

mp

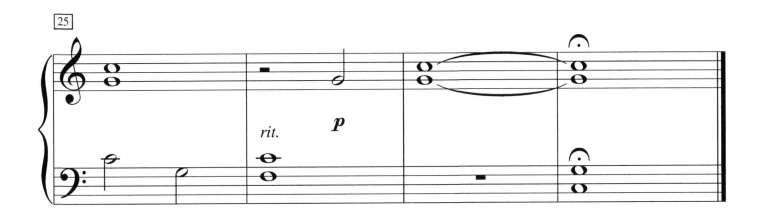

rit. *p*

I WILL FOLLOW

Words and Music by CHRIS TOMLIN,
REUBEN MORGAN and JASON INGRAM
Arranged by Phillip Keveren

Decisively (♩ = 100)

mf All Your ways are good, ___ all Your ways are sure. ___ I will

trust in You ___ a - lone. ___ High - er than my sight, ___ high a - bove my life, ___

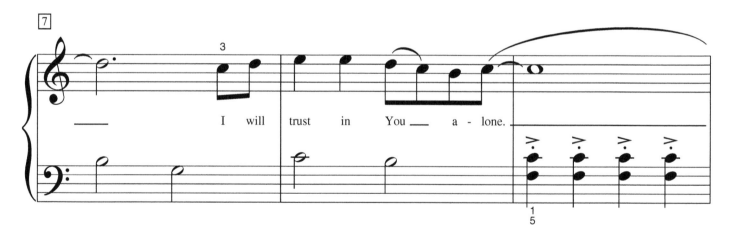

___ I will trust in You ___ a - lone.

___ *f* Where You go, I'll go. ___ Where You stay, I'll stay. ___

When You move, I'll move. I will fol - low You. Who You love, I'll love.

How You serve, I'll serve. If this life I lose, I will fol - low You,

yeah. I will fol - low You, yeah.

I will fol - low You, *rit.* yeah.

INDESCRIBABLE

Words and Music by LAURA STORY
and JESSE REEVES
Arranged by Phillip Keveren

Flowing, in one (♩ = 176)

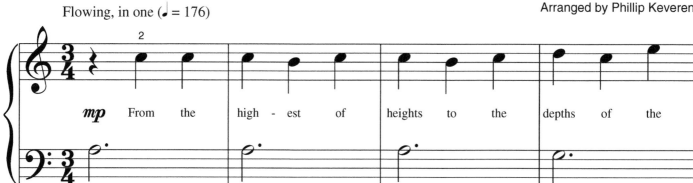

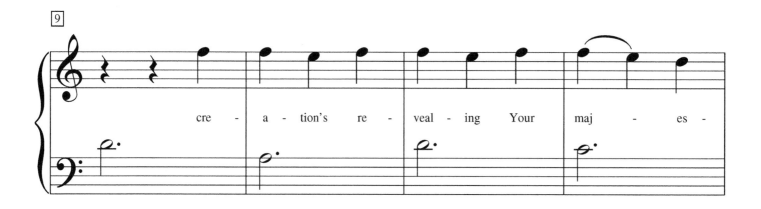

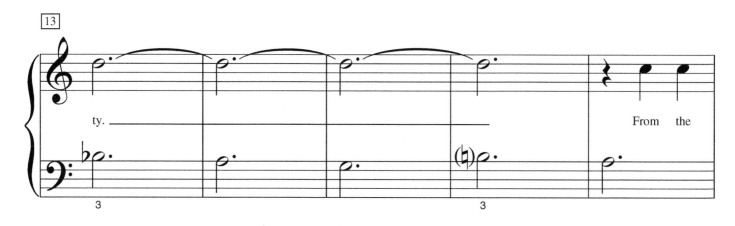

col - ors of fall to the fra - grance of spring, _____

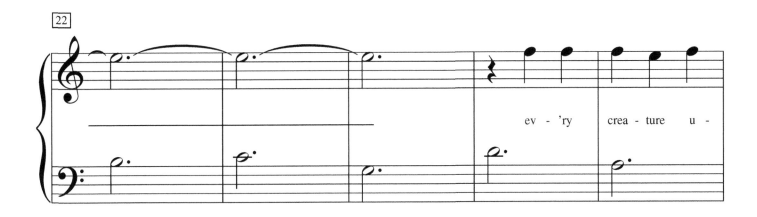

_____ ev - 'ry crea - ture u -

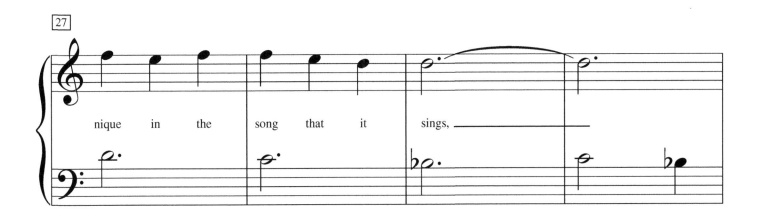

nique in the song that it sings, _____

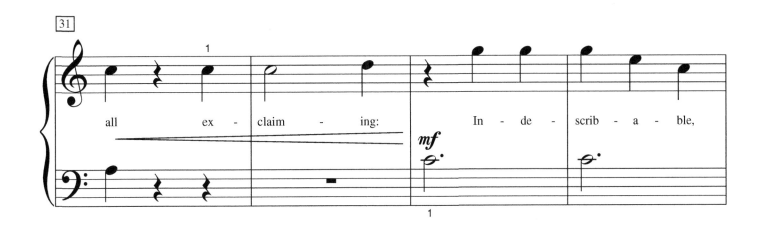

all ex - claim - ing: In - de - scrib - a - ble,

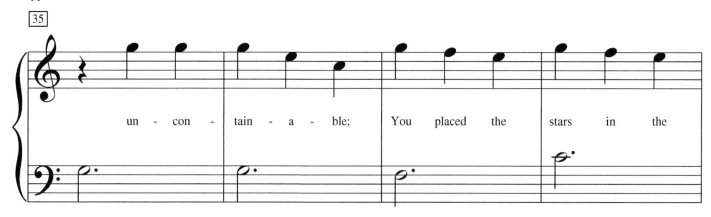

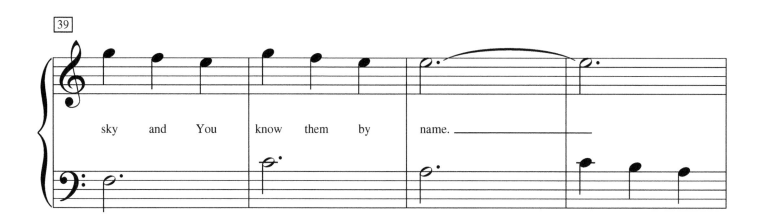

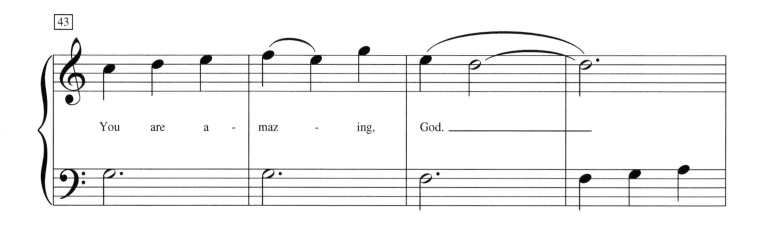

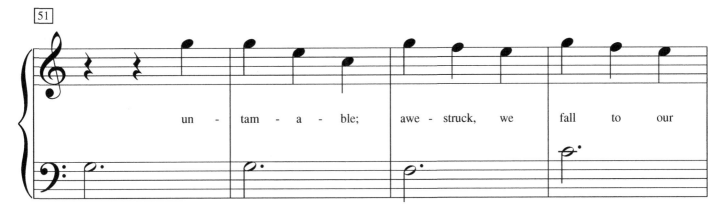

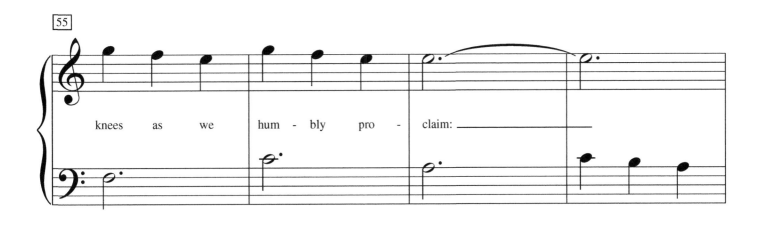

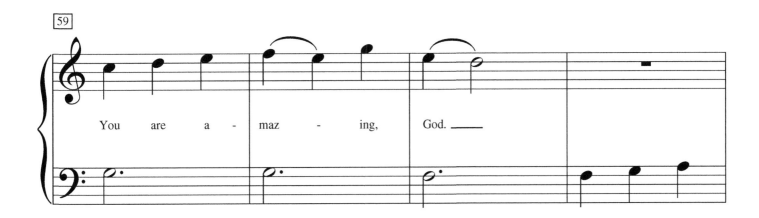

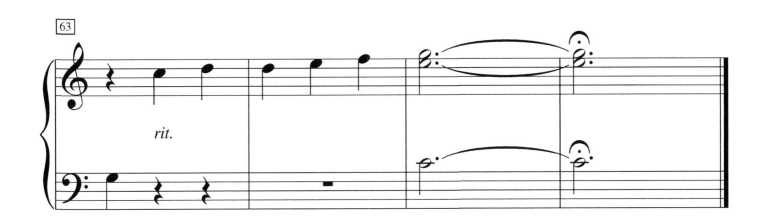

OFFERING

Words and Music by
PAUL BALOCHE
Arranged by Phillip Keveren

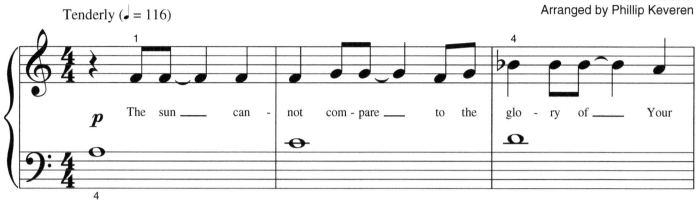

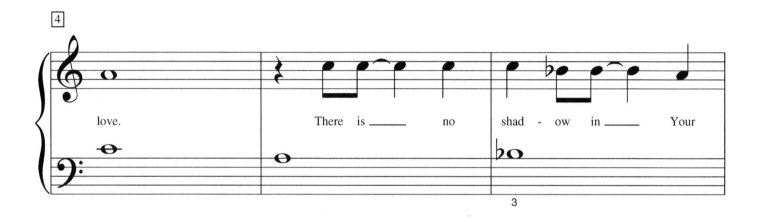

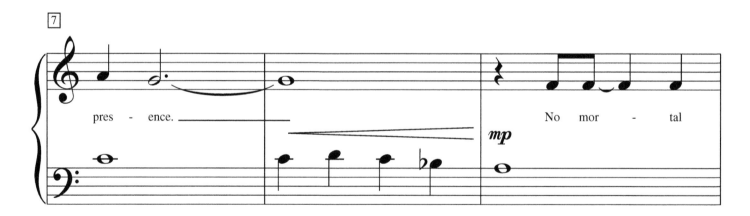

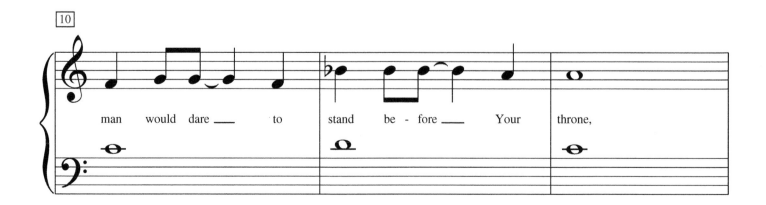

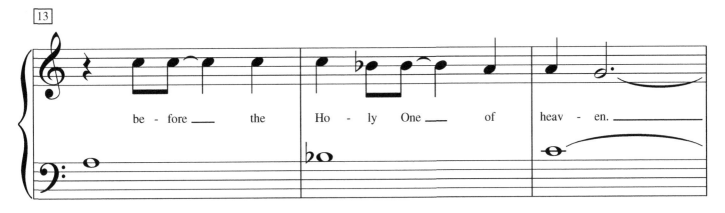

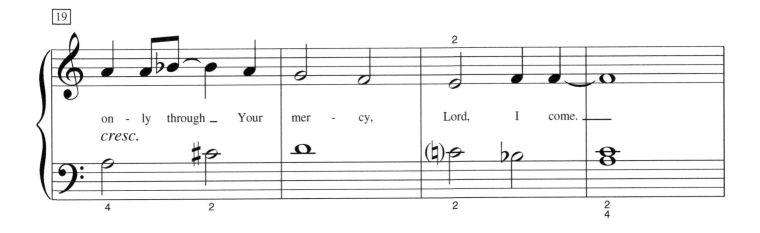

King.

No one on earth de - serves ___ the

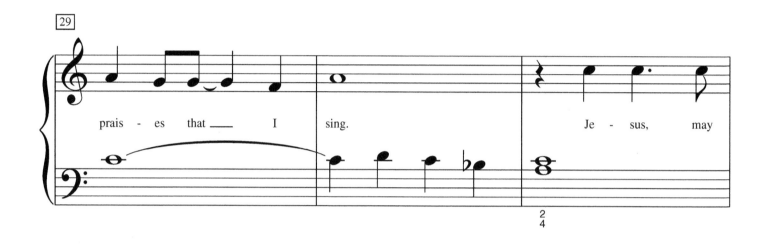

prais - es that ___ I sing.

Je - sus, may

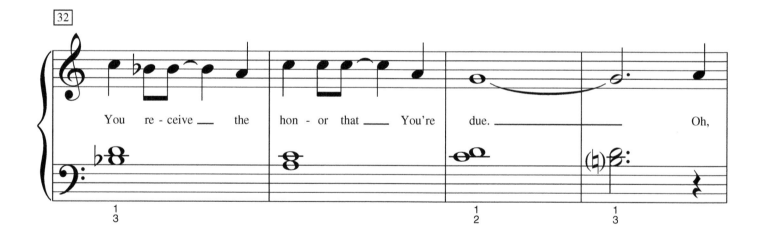

You re - ceive ___ the hon - or that ___ You're due. _____ Oh,

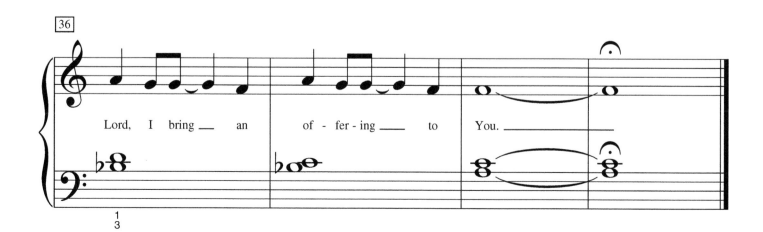

Lord, I bring ___ an of - fer - ing ___ to You. _____

SING TO THE KING

Words and Music by
BILLY JAMES FOOTE
Arranged by Phillip Keveren

Spirited (♩ = 126)

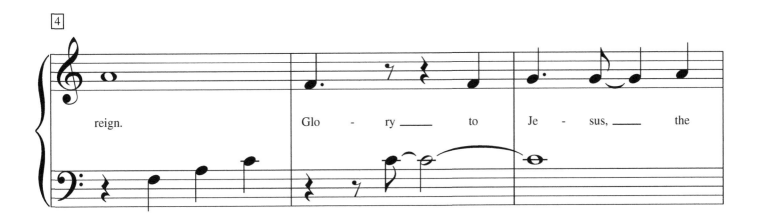

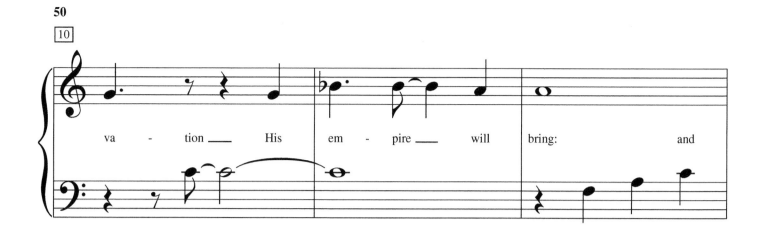

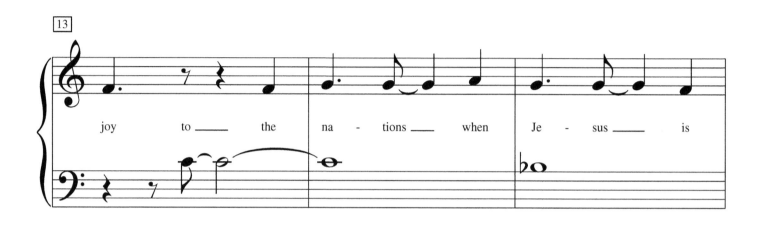

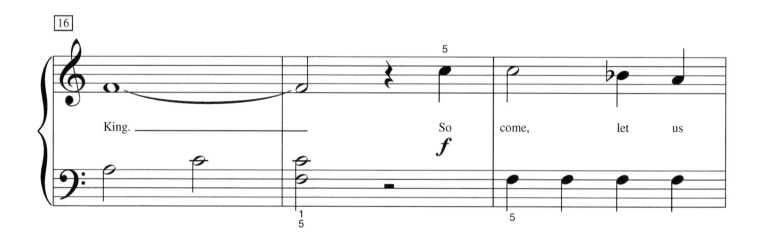

Je - sus; _____ and He's all we need.

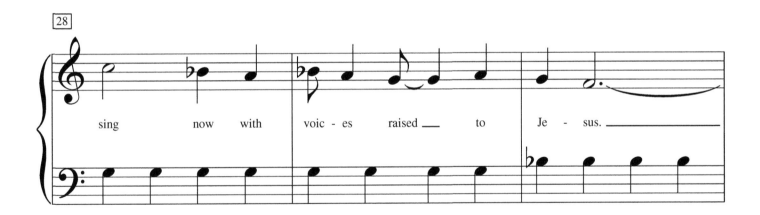

Lift up a heart of praise, __

sing now with voic - es raised __ to Je - sus. _____

__ Sing to the King!

1
5

REVELATION SONG

Words and Music by
JENNIE LEE RIDDLE
Arranged by Phillip Keveren

Reverently (♩ = 69)

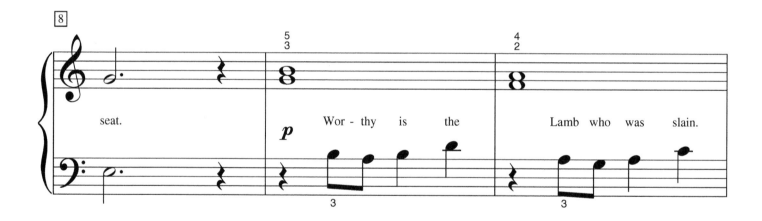

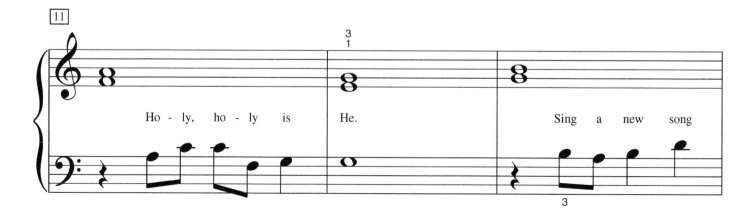

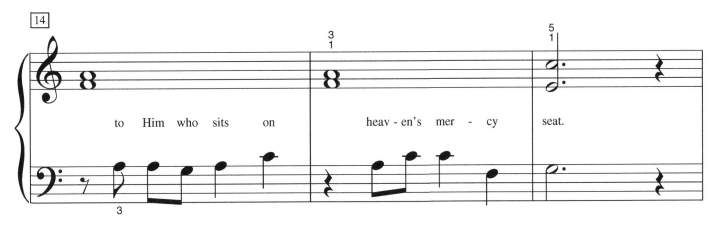

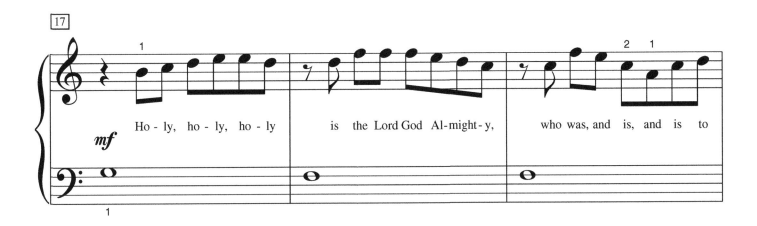

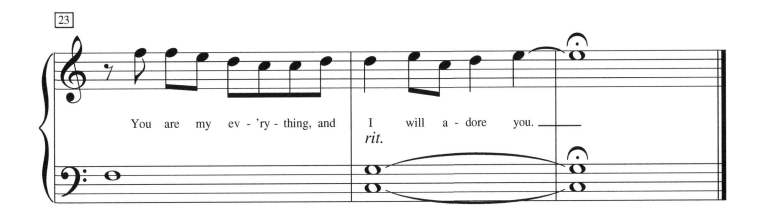

YOUR GRACE IS ENOUGH

Words and Music by
MATT MAHER
Arranged by Phillip Keveren

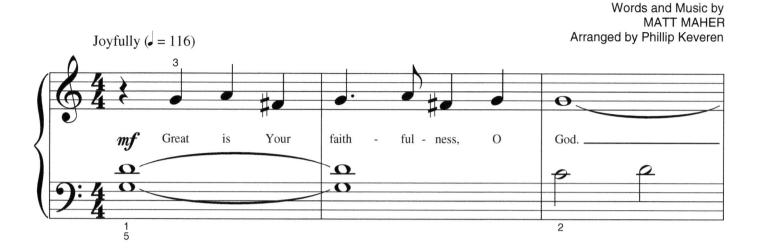

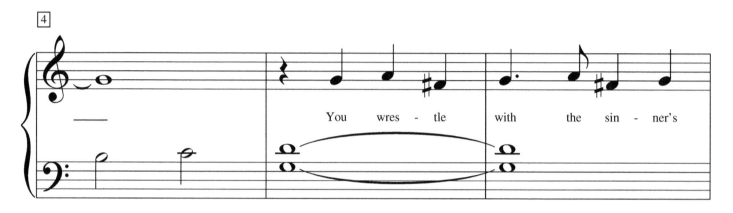

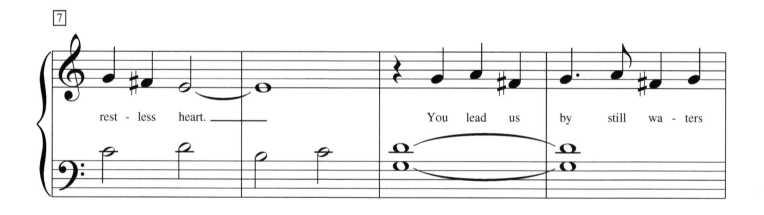

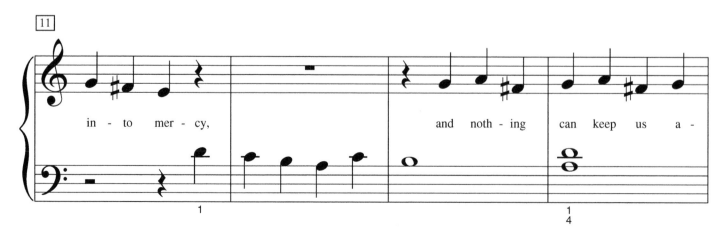

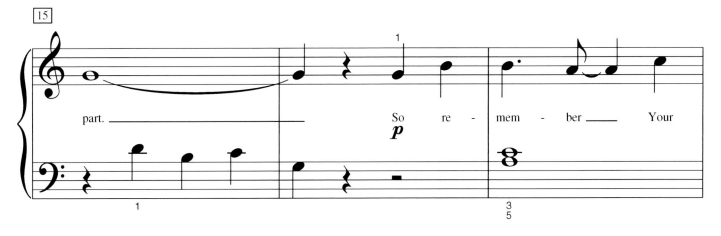

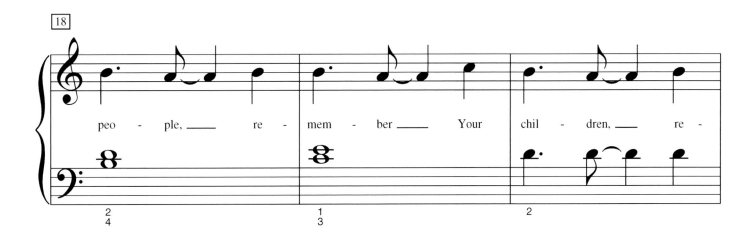

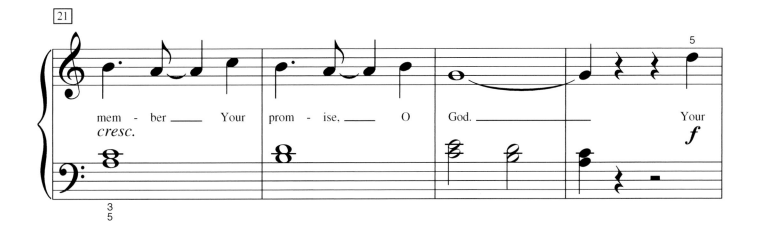

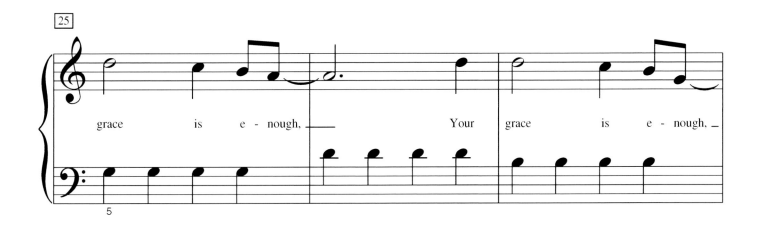

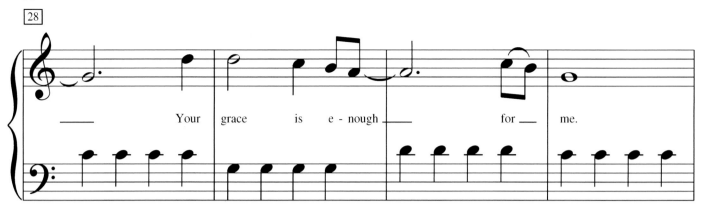

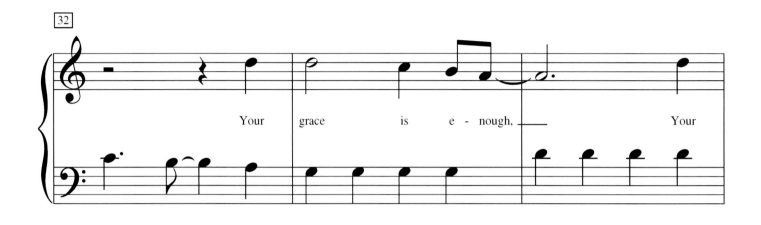

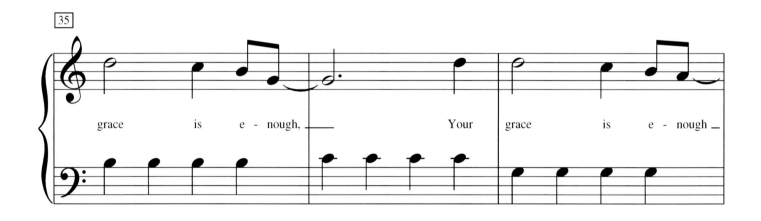

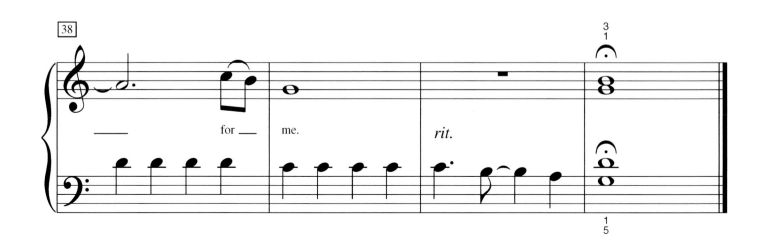